Yosemite National Park Tour Guide Book

By Waypoint Tours

Front Cover - Upper & Lower Yosemite Falls Reflections

Back Cover - Half Dome Sunset from Glacier Point

Contents

Tour Maps	Page 4
1) Yosemite	Page 8
2) Bridalveil Fall W1	Page 12
3) El Capitan & Bridalveil View V14	Page 14
4) Sentinel Rock & Four-Mile Trail V18	Page 16
5) Sentinel Bridge & Cooks Meadow	Page 18
6) Curry Village V22	Page 22
7) Happy Isles & Waterfalls V24	Page 24
8) Stoneman Meadow & Royal Arches V23	Page 26
9) Yosemite Village V1	Page 28
10) Ahwahnee Lodge	Page 30
11) Yosemite Falls V3	Page 32
12) Tunnel View W2	Page 36
13) Chinquapin W5	Page 38
14) Glacier Point G11	Page 40
15) Wawona W10	Page 42
16) Mariposa Grove S1	Page 44
17) Tuolumne Grove O1	Page 46
18) Olmsted Point & Tenaya Lake T24	Page 48
19) Tuolumne Meadows T29	Page 50
20) Tioga Pass & Lakes T39	Page 52
21) Mirror Lake V26	Page 54
22) Hetch Hetchy H4	Page 56
23) San Francisco	Page 58
24) San Francisco Wharf & Maritime Park	Page 60
Optional CD & DVD Info	Page 63

W1, W14, etc. Correspond to
Park Roadside Markers

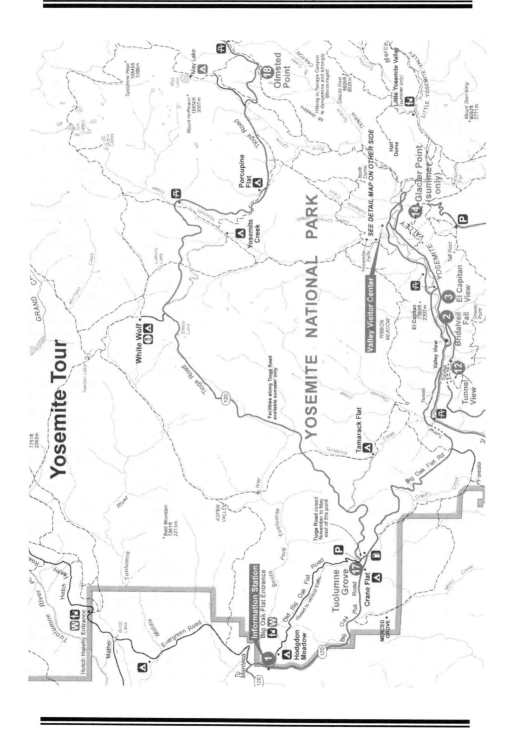

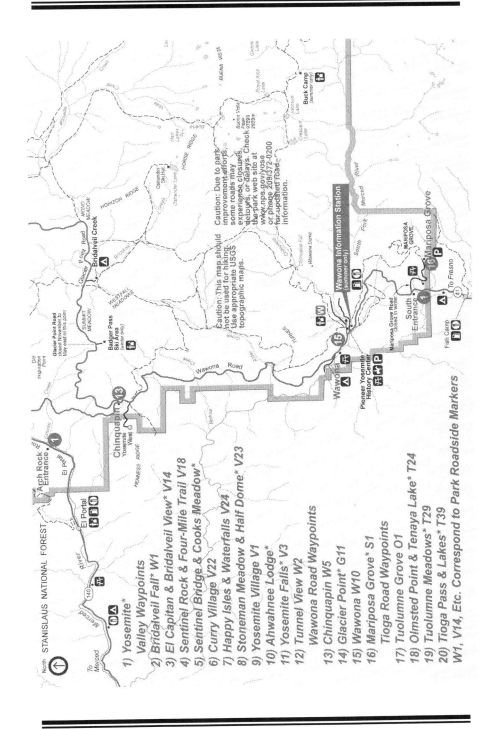

1) Yosemite*
   Valley Waypoints
2) Bridalveil Fall* W1
3) El Capitan & Bridalveil View* V14
4) Sentinel Rock & Four-Mile Trail V18
5) Sentinel Bridge & Cooks Meadow*
6) Curry Village V22
7) Happy Isles & Waterfalls V24
8) Stoneman Meadow & Half Dome* V23
9) Yosemite Village V1
10) Ahwahnee Lodge*
11) Yosemite Falls* V3
12) Tunnel View W2
    Wawona Road Waypoints
13) Chinquapin W5
14) Glacier Point* G11
15) Wawona W10
16) Mariposa Grove* S1
    Tioga Road Waypoints
17) Tuolumne Grove O1
18) Olmsted Point & Tenaya Lake* T24
19) Tuolumne Meadows* T29
20) Tioga Pass & Lakes* T39
W1, V14, Etc. Correspond to Park Roadside Markers

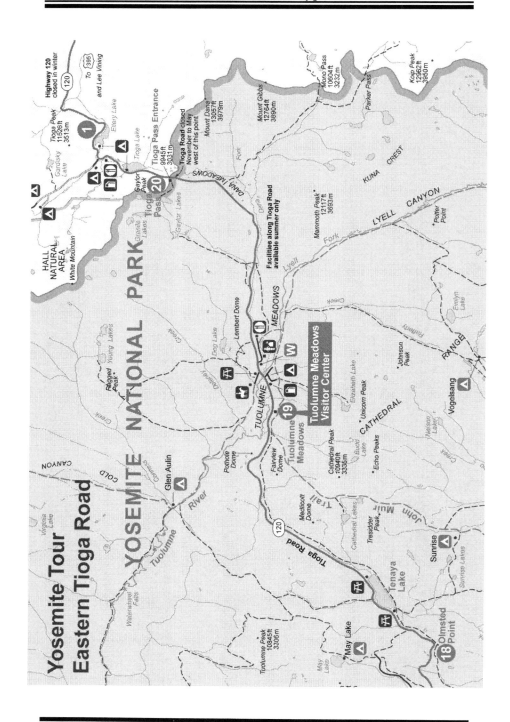

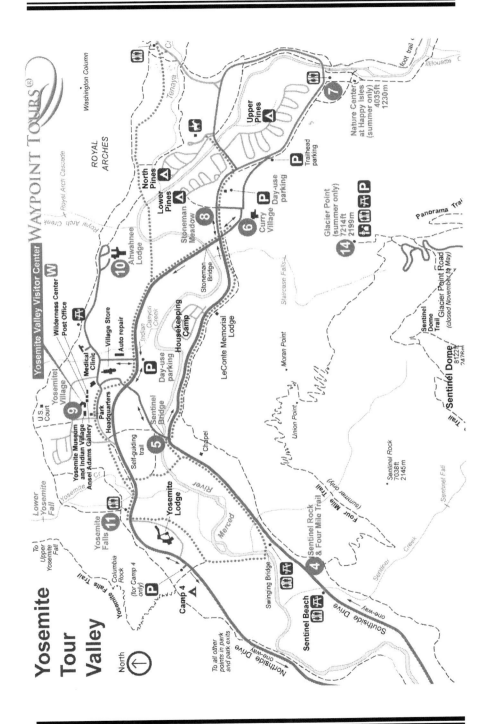

1) Yosemite

Welcome to Yosemite's 1,170 square miles of light, height and depth. The highest peak in Yosemite National Park is Mount Lyell, 13,114 feet above sea level. Yosemite Valley is nearly a mile deep, with a 3,000-foot vertical drop at El Capitan. Of the 13 waterfalls in Yosemite Valley, two are among the world's top 10 tallest, Yosemite Falls at 2,425 feet and Sentinel Falls at 2,000 feet.

We hope this Yosemite tour will deepen your understanding of the forces of nature which created John Muir's "Range of Light," heighten your awareness of Yosemite's ecosystems, and intrigue you with its history. Join us as we embark on the adventure of exploring Yosemite, past and present.

Yosemite became a National Park in 1890, 200 million years after the granite rocks formed within the earth; 20,000 years after glaciers eroded the gritty granite; 4,000 years after Ahwahneechee Indians were caretakers of the meadows; 2,000 years after Grizzly Giant, one of the largest and oldest sequoias was a seedling; and 41 years after gold was discovered in California.

The rugged geography of Yosemite Valley kept it secret and isolated for many years. Only in 1851, when early miners and settlers felt their livelihood threatened by Indians, and vice versa, did white man intrude upon the valley.

To some, Yosemite is a place to check off their list - sights to be seen or mountaineering routes to scale; for others, Yosemite is a destination of solitude, peace, and escape. With the large number of people visiting the valley each year, how do you avoid the crowds at peak times and find the true beauty of Yosemite?

Change. Change your timing and your focus. You can stay on the beaten paths, but travel them early or late in the day, or find the trails less traveled. While others are looking up, cameras clicking to capture the familiar falls and formations, change your focus to find what they are missing - the fragile ferns at your feet, the black and white crystals peppering the rocks, or the ripple in the stream.

John Muir instructed: "Climb the mountains and get their good tidings. Nature's peace will flow into you as sunshine flows into trees. The winds will blow their own freshness into you, and the storms their energy, while cares will drop off like autumn leaves."

Top - Tioga Lake Reflections
Bottom - Valley View with El Capitan,
*   Half Dome & Bridalveil Fall*
Page 10 - Tioga Pass Entrance &
*   El Portal Arch Rock Entrance*
Page 11 - Top of Bridalveil Fall &
*   Vernal Falls at Happy Isles*

2) Bridalveil Fall W1

The rainbows created by the blowing mist of Bridalveil Fall are beautiful to behold. In 1856, the water falling freely 620 feet over the precipice, was blown by a breeze, caught the light, and reminded Warren Baer, editor of the Mariposa Democrat, of a bride's veil, and so he named it.

The Miwok Indians, however, called it "Po-ho-no," "The Spirit of the Evil Wind." According to one of their legends, a fair Indian maiden, gathering berries along the top of the fall, was entranced by the rainbow and mists. She drew close to the edge to observe the beauty and then was blown over it by a stiff wind. The old Indian chief warned that no one should venture again within the mists, as it was the home of Po-ho-no, who would hold them captive in his dank abode.

Pohono or not, care should be taken if you walk the short trail to the base of the fall; the rocks can be slippery when wet. The tumbling water, crashing into the large granodiorite boulders at the base of the fall, spawns waves of mist, which diffract the light and create the amazing rainbows for which the fall is known.

To obtain the best rainbow pictures, stand before the mist with the sun at your back when it is low in the sky, such as early morning or evening. Although the Bridalveil is at its best in spring and early summer, excellent pictures can be taken at other times of year as well because this fall does not dry up in the autumn.

The steady water supply encourages a variety of plants at the base of Bridalveil Fall, and also attracts a wide range of wildlife. Beneath the incense cedar, ponderosa pine, oak, big-leaf maples and alders, the Miwoks hunted deer, squirrels, quail, and rabbits. They also ate manzanita berries, gooseberries, currants, wild strawberries and elderberries. Wild rose hips and leaves were used to make a soothing tea. The leaves and roots of nettles were used to reduce rheumatism and as an antiseptic, analgesic and coagulant. Many of the uses for nettles have since been confirmed by clinical studies. And just in case the Indians ate too many berries, a tea made from monkey flower roots could be used to relieve those symptoms as well.

3) El Capitan & Bridalveil View V14

El Capitan rises with glorious nobility over 3,000 feet from the valley floor. Tips of ponderosa pines, dwarfed by its immensity, point upward to the shear escarpment which glows with reflected sunlight

Indian legend, called El Capitan Too-Tock-Awn-oo-Lah after the inchworm who slowly but surely was able to scale the steep cliff. If you look closely, you may see modern day adventurous counterparts who come from all walks of life - teachers, scientists, moms and dads, as well as college kids - inch their way up the mountain.

The first complete climb of El Capitan by the Nose Route was in 1958 by Warren Harding. Thirty-five years later, Lynn Hills did the first free climb of the original Nose Route and in 1999, Mark Wellman was the first paraplegic to scale the heights. Climbing techniques have advanced significantly; nylon rope and Kevlar slings have replaced hemp rope and for those that practice "clean climbing," "chocks," "friends," and "cams" have replaced bolts, "pitons," and chiseled holds.

The unusual names of routes up the rock escarpments come from whoever completes the "first ascent" for each particular route.

One can only imagine what they were thinking when they named some of the over 70 routes on El Capitan, such names as "Realm of the Flying Monkeys," "Lurking Fear," "New Jersey Turnpike," "Eagles Way," and "Lost World." Typical rock climbing routes consist of 1 to 30 "pitches" which are equivalent to 50 feet of rope, but the climbing challenges in Yosemite are often a multi-day affair using techniques pioneered by John Salathe on Lost Arrow Chimney and Sentinel Rock. The average time to climb El Capitan is four days, but seven to nine days is more common. The firefly glow of climbers hanging in their cocoons for the night off the sheer cliffs is truly an astounding sight to see.

El Capitan was not the first Granite Megalith to be tackled. In 1875, George Anderson made the first ascent of Half Dome. Across from El Capitan are Cathedral Rocks and the 1,900 and 2,100 foot tall Cathedral Spires which were climbed in 1933.

El Capitan's massive size is due to a lack of joints in the granite at that location. However, at the Three Brothers formation, a unique set of parallel joints which angle toward the surface break up the El Capitan granite and create the three peaks named after Chief Tenaya's sons who were captured near there during the second expedition of the Mariposa Battalion in 1851.

The Three Brothers formation lived up to its Indian name, Waw-haw-kee, for "falling rocks." In 1987, a rock slide at Middle Brother generated 1.4 million tons of rock which rumbled all the way down to the Merced River. You can tell which rocks come from rock slides by their angularity and similarity to the cliffs above and which were left behind by glaciers, such as the rocks of the El Capitan Moraine, characterized by more rounded features and distinctness from nearby rocks.

4) Sentinel Rock & Four-Mile Trail V18

Keeping watch over Yosemite Valley is the 3,073 foot tall Sentinel Rock. The massive "cookies and cream" colored granodiorite formation guarded the first permanent structure in the valley, the Lower Hotel, built at its base in 1856. The Upper Hotel, later called the Hutching's House, was built two to three years later, just up the road, in what was to become the "Old Village."

James Mason Hutchings led the first "tourist" party to the valley in 1855, and promoted the valley by publishing Thomas Ayres' sketches of the "incomparable" valley. Hutchings had a long history with Yosemite, including succeeding Galen Clark as Yosemite's Guardian in 1880, and building a sawmill which John Muir ran for a period of time.

Development in Yosemite Valley accelerated with the opening of the Coulterville Road and the Big Oak Flat Roads in 1874. Paying a toll and riding in a bumpy wagon down the steep switchbacks may have been rough, but many considered it an improvement over riding horseback. In the early 1870's, James McCauley had John Conway build the original "Four-Mile Trail" from the base of Sentinel Rock to his "Mountain House" at Glacier Point. This trail is still known for its awe-inspiring vistas of the valley and waterfalls.

By the late 1800's, when the Yosemite Chapel was built at the base of Sentinel Rock, there were multiple hotels around the Valley. Initially, the area's fresh produce needs were met by one man, James Lamon, Yosemite Valley's first homesteader, but many settlers kept coming to the valley.

As civilization continued to encroach upon the once-pristine area, bringing a sawmill, livestock, crops, orchards, fences, and outbuildings, Yosemite Valley began to lose the awe-inspiring appeal of nature that drew tourists here in the first place. To protect the area, Congress passed an act establishing Yosemite National Park in 1890 and dispatched cavalry troops from the Presidio in San Francisco to help enforce it.

By 1907, the Yosemite Valley Railroad was built between Merced and El Portal, which brought more tourists. The first automobile entered the valley in 1900, and in 1926 the "All-Year Highway," was built by convict labor. The highway increased the use of cars and had a heavy impact on the railroad's revenue leading to its eventual closure in 1945.

The "Old Village" in Yosemite Valley continued to grow however, and Yosemite Chapel was moved to the "Old Village." The "Old Village" also boasted photography studios, a general store, post office, park headquarters, hotels, saloons, residences, and a dancing pavilion. Eventually, construction shifted to the north side of the valley in the "New Village."

By the late 1960's, Glacier Point's Mountain House and most of the "Old Village" structures had either burned down, been demolished, or moved to Pioneer Village in Wawona. Only the Yosemite Chapel remains as a testament to the beginning of the tourist boon, which has grown to millions of visitors annually.

5) Sentinel Bridge & Cooks Meadow

At Sentinel Bridge, there is a wonderful view of Half Dome, framed by the trees lining the Merced River. In 1806, Spanish Sergeant Gabriel Moraga was so relieved to see water while crossing the dry San Joaquin Valley, he named this river, "El Rio de Nuestra Senora de la Merced" - The River of Our Lady of Mercy. The river, today simply known as the Merced, originates in the snowfields of the High Sierras, and drops over 11,000 feet on its way to the Pacific Ocean.

While the Merced is a quiet river that accommodates photographers by providing moving reflections of the valley's magnificent domes and waterfalls, she is also known to have a temper. In January 1997, heavy flooding did significant damage to manmade structures and roads, and closed the valley to tourism for three months.

Flooding, however, is an important element for the preservation of certain habitats. Fresh emergent wetlands and wet meadows are important for hydrophytes, water-loving plants which contribute rich nutrients to the ecologic system. They also provide breeding areas for western toads and Pacific tree frogs. Mallards and red-winged blackbirds also frequently nest in emergent wetlands.

In the summer, when the river is typically in a tranquil mood, valley visitors enjoy swimming and wading in the cool water. While relaxing on the river beaches, they may see the blue crown of a belted kingfisher as he carefully watches the river ripples for the delicate dance of a rainbow trout's fins. To catch fish or insects, the kingfisher dives headfirst into the water.

His human counterparts, however, must use catch and release fishing with artificial lures for rainbow trout, the only native game fish in Yosemite. Brown trout, an introduced species, is more abundant and today's fishermen can keep those when caught, up to a reasonable limit.

Rainbow trout was a mainstay of the Miwok diet and they were caught by hand, nets, baskets and spears. The ingenious Indians also found an even more efficient way to fish, by mixing pulverized soaproot into slower moving water. This resulted in the fish becoming stupefied which caused them to float up to the surface, where they could be easily scooped up.

As you look across the idyllic river and the blossoms dance in a breeze, realize that this abundance is responsible for hiding voles, supporting deer and bears, and providing seed grasses for sparrows, jays, and tanagers.

Then imagine what it looked like 500 years ago. Indian boys may have been playing "skinny," a game where a ball, similar in size to a baseball, was hit with clubs between field goals. The women may have been gathering willow, maple, hazel, pine, oak, redbud, deer brush or squaw bush to make simple twined baskets coated with soaproot juice to be used for seed gathering, or else gathering the slender twigs of Coulter pine to make intricate, beautiful coiled baskets for gathering acorns or serving food.

6) Curry Village V22

As you stand beneath the picturesque entrance sign of Camp Curry, where Mother Curry herself once stood to greet visitors in 1899, it is not difficult to imagine this camp in its heyday.

Imagine it is 1967, 9 p.m. on a cool summer evening in Yosemite, the last summer of the Firefall. The crowd gathers expectantly at Camp Curry, at Ahwahnee, in the meadows, and at Glacier Point. The lights go out in the valley right on time.

In Camp Curry, all eyes are on the emissary on stage, who shouts: "Halll-ll-ooooo Gla-aaa-cierrrr Pooiiinnnt!"

Everyone's head tilts back as they look up and anticipate the response: "Halll-llll-oooo Caaaammmmp Curr-rrrraaaayy!"

Then from Camp Curry, a potent pause and the command: "Let the fiii-iire fa-aa-aaallll!"

Followed by the final reassurance from above: "The fiii-yuuuure falllls!"

Suddenly, over the precipice of Glacier Point tumbles glowing embers of red fir bark, accompanied by a tinkling, almost bell-like sound as everyone sits in silent, reverent awe. Then the song, "Indian Love Call," hauntingly drifts from the Camp Curry stage as the embers slowly fade in their graceful descent.

The memories last a lifetime for those who saw it. For those who sat in the bleachers and watched bears raid the garbage dump under spotlights, those memories also last a lifetime. Both events are gone now.

Also gone is the miniature train at Camp Curry, the miniature golf course at the Ahwahnee, and the "Indian Field Days" rodeo, but endangered species, such as the bighorn sheep and peregrine falcons are making a comeback. Rock climbers helped by ferrying fragile falcon eggs, thinned by pesticide residue the birds accidentally ingested, from the nests to an incubation staff that helped hatch them. Meanwhile, the unsuspecting parents sat on plastic egg substitutes until climbers ferried newborn chicks back to the nest. In 2003, there were four nesting pairs of peregrine falcons in Yosemite and they were taken off the endangered list.

Grizzly bears were not so fortunate and have not been found in Yosemite since 1895. Black bears are prevalent, however, and are undergoing reconditioning programs to break the chain of dependency on tourist-supplied foods. Black bears have to eat 20,000 calories daily to prepare for winter. That is 1,650 acorns or 130 chocolate bars! Fewer of these magnificent bears are now being put down for unfavorable human interaction because of the rental of bear canisters and educational programs which promote park stewardship.

The name black bear is a bit of a misnomer because their coats can actually be brown, cinnamon, or even blonde. No matter what the color of their coat, however, it is better to see a 250 to 500 pound bear across a meadow than it is in your campsite looking for chocolate bars!

7) Happy Isles & Waterfalls V24

River and fen, forest and talus, combine to create a shady, cool realm of enchantment named the Happy Isles in 1885 by W.E. Dennison, who was then Guardian of the Yosemite Grant. In the spring, even the animals appear to be happy here alongside the tumbling, singing Merced River as it bounds exuberantly over Nevada and Vernal Falls, playfully surrounds the islands, and dances joyfully over the boulders of granodiorite on its way to the wide valley beyond. Chipmunks scamper quickly among the ferns, their striped backs and masked faces helping to define which of the six subspecies in Yosemite they belong. The white spots of the mule deer fawns and the puma or mountain lion cubs help them blend into the forest dappled with sunlight filtering through the trees. A quiet stroll along the boardwalk in the cool peat-forming wetlands of the fen is a magnificent way to experience the natural enchantment of Happy Isles.

As spring turns to summer, the sun highlights the wisps of the beautiful Illiouette Fall, and it warms the needle triplets of the ponderosa pine, causing the sweet vanilla-butterscotch fragranced sap to ooze out between the large puzzle-like plates of bark on the stout trunks. The chickadees, nuthatches, and flickers gather along streams to sing. The delightful warble coming from the black, white and orange-marked grosbeak is a welcome contrast to the raucous caw of the black brazen raven or brilliant blue Steller's jay's screech. Bird-watchers from all over the world come to Yosemite in hopes of catching a glimpse of the Gray-crowned Rosy Finch, Williamson's Sapsucker, the Black Swift, Peregrine Falcon, Northern Groshawk, and various owls including the Great Gray Owl, Flammulated Owl and Northern Pygmy Owl. Although a massive rockslide damaged the Visitor Center at Happy Isles in 1996, it has been repaired and has excellent interactive displays on the local habitats and the animals and birds thriving in them.

In the fall, the Nevada and Vernal Falls reward adventurous hikers who traipse the shady trails. California gray squirrels rustle in the fallen golden-red leaves of the large California black oaks and ferret away the acorns to store for the coming winter. Acorn woodpeckers are also diligently storing away acorns in each hole they have drilled in trees, telephone poles and even buildings. If you look closely, you may also see Black-backed and large, 15-inch Pileated Woodpeckers. Goldenrods, lupines and asters decorate the more open areas and the cool, clean air ripples through golden willows, alders, cottonwoods, and reddened maples and oaks.

In the quiet white of winter, the ermine's white fur blends in as it stalks its prey beneath the yellow flowering incense cedar, deep green boughs of Douglas-fir, and holly-like leaves of Canyon live oak. Hoof prints and paw prints give away the quiet passing of mule deer, coyote, and mountain lions. The quiet is interrupted with the floompf of snow falling from a branch as the Douglas squirrels bound among the branches, the tufts on their ears readily apparent in winter.

Occasionally rockslides and avalanches can be heard as the weight of the snow increases beyond the endurance limit of the rock edifices weakened by freezing and thawing in their joints. You can tell the direction of the flow of rock or snow avalanches based on the direction of knocked-down pine trees pointing their tips downstream like arrows. Come spring, all things will be made new again, and the fresh talus slopes will become home to more wild creatures.

Happy Isles Visitor Center & Vernal Falls

8) Stoneman Meadow & Royal Arches V23

This meadow provides one of the best views of Half Dome, boldly rising 4,748 feet above the valley floor, with Tissack's forlorn face looking longingly towards Mono Lake, darkly etched on the fractured stone. The Indian legend of Tissack is a tale of love and anger. An Ahwahneechee brave traveled to Mono Lake and brought back with him a beautiful bride, Tissack. Although she thought the valley was lovely, she missed her home. She tried to run back to Mono Lake but her husband stopped her. The basket on her back and baby's cradle were thrown aside and became Basket Dome and the Royal Arches. Because of their anger, she and her husband were also turned to stone. He became North Dome, and her face, with its trail of tears, became permanently imprinted on Half Dome, a reminder to keep anger at bay and maintain the peace and tranquility of the valley.

The term "embattled wilderness" is sometimes used to describe the attempt to balance tourist needs with preservation of the wilderness, which has been an on-going struggle from the very beginning. In 1886, the State of California built the Stoneman House in this meadow to provide improved housing for tourists. The hotel burned down in 1896 however, leaving an open and unencumbered view.

As you peer across the meadow, with monarch butterflies, robins, red-winged blackbirds, and Brewer's blackbirds flying above golden dots of black-eyed susans, goldenrod and yarrow amongst the green grasses, cow parsnip, bull thistle and milkweed, notice how the shape of the Royal Arches is mirrored in the curvature of North Dome above it.

This area was once covered by rolling hillsides and a gentle meandering river. These were eroded away and the underlying granite tried to relieve the stresses pent up inside by expanding outward. Granite is so strong, however, that the stress builds up until it literally tears itself apart, forming cracks or joints in the rock which are parallel to the surface. So, underneath a hill, the crack will arch upward as you see in the Royal Arches. Then, the shell-like layers formed by the cracks spall off, leaving a dome. The imprint of the prior landscape is forever captured. Soaring domes and a magnificent glaciated chasm now stand where once rolling hillsides and a gentle river meandered.

Kenneth Brower stated it well when he wrote in the National Geographic Yosemite: "The forms in it, the ancient landscape, were all unrealized, like the "David" before Michelangelo freed it from the marble."

Washington Column, so named because its profile as viewed from the four-mile trail is thought to resemble the first president, formed from vertical joints which also appear in the rocks. Half Dome's unique shape was originally thought to have been formed by cracking along vertical joints and then losing half its mass to the glaciers which carved the valley. Actually, about 80% of Half Dome is still there; its unusual profile due more to the shape of the granite pluton from which it formed.

Top - Half Dome
Bottom - Royal Arches, North Dome & Washington Column

9) Yosemite Village V1

In the early 1920's, David Hull, the Park Service's senior landscape engineer, chose a spot for Yosemite Village, the "New Village," which was less susceptible to flooding and on the side of the valley which receives more warmth and sunlight than the "Old Village." The new Post Office, Museum and Administration building, and Rangers' Club had a rustic rough-hewn style which would come to typify the "Arts and Crafts Movement" of architecture in National Park Service buildings. Also seen in the historic areas of Yosemite Village are examples of early U.S. Army buildings, and the modernistic Mission 66-style buildings, such as the Tourist Center, built for the National Park Service's 50th anniversary.

The renovated Yosemite Visitor Center, with its excellent displays and introductory movies, is well worth a visit. Many visitors also stop to check out the tree rings on a slice of a 1,000 year old Sequoia tree at the front of the Yosemite Museum; but, even greater treasures await the discerning traveler inside the museum, including historic books, herbarium, famous photographs, artwork, and artifacts such as traditional Indian dress made of flicker, magpie, crow, turkey vulture, or western red tail hawk feathers. Eagle feathers were not used because they were believed to bring bad luck.

Located near the Museum and Visitor Center is the Indian Village with native structures such as acorn granaries, called chakkas and a sweathouse, called a tcapu'ya where the braves prepared for hunting expeditions.

Preliminary evidence, gathered from the thousands of archaeological sites in the park, indicates that native people may have been living in the Sierras for as long as 9,500 years. It is generally accepted that they occupied the valley itself for over 4,000 years. Diseases brought by immigration of other native peoples, displaced from along the coastal areas in the early 1800's by the Spanish, combined with natural influences such as drought, earthquakes or floods, may have caused them to leave the valley.

Among those to flee was a young Miwok chief who went to live with the Mono Lake Piautes, married and had a son, Tenaya. Tenaya lead a band of Indians, made up of several different tribes, back to the valley to reclaim his birthright. They were known by many names, including "uzumati," for grizzly bears, because of their bravery and skill, even when faced, weaponless, with the grizzly bear himself. Some believe "Yosemite" is a derivation of "uzumati."

When Major Savage and the Mariposa Battallion entered Yosemite Valley in 1851, in retaliation for Indian raids on their settlements and Savage's Trading Post, the Indians living here were most likely a mixture of Miwoks, Paiutes, and Yokuts. In the ensuing two years, Tenaya's tribe spent time on an Indian reservation at Mono Lake, and even some time back in their cherished valley, but after Tenaya died in 1853, the tribe no longer had the same cohesiveness or spirit.

10) Ahwahnee Lodge

Beneath the Royal Arches are accommodations fit for royalty. The Ahwahnee Hotel, designed by Gilbert Stanley Underwood and decorated with museum-quality native Indian Miwok and Mono artifacts and kelim and soumak tapestries from the Middle East, hosted Queen Elizabeth and Prince Philip in 1983. Since its opening in 1927, the guestbook has been a veritable guide to Who's Who in history - Herbert Hoover, Franklin and Eleanor Roosevelt, Winston Churchill, Dwight Eisenhower, John Kennedy, and Ronald Reagan. Rich and famous celebrities, including Desi Arnez, Lucille Ball, Judy Garland, Shirley Temple, Helen Hayes, Jack Benny, and Red Skelton have also stayed at the Ahwahnee.

When the U.S. Navy needed a convalescent hospital during World War II, the Ahwahnee was host to over 850 sailors, nurses, doctors and other staff. Naval officers occupied the Tressider Suite and the Great Lounge was a dormitory for the men and women who cared for the recovering sailors housed in the accompanying wings. The Tressider Suite was named for Donald B. Tresidder, son-in-law of "Mother" Jenny Curry, former president of the Yosemite Park and Curry Company, and former president of Stanford University.

Stephen Tyng Mather, a wealthy businessman who was also an outdoorsman and member of the Sierra Club, had the right combination of negotiating skills, foresight, contacts and passion to overcome obstacles and not only build the Ahwahnee Hotel, but also to form the National Park Service. In Mather's vision, the National Parks would be available to people of every economic level.

Lodges, such as the Ahwahnee, would provide places where those accustomed to comfort, and with the ability to influence congressional funding, could experience the rustic beauty of the parks in an elegant way. Through the influence of the affluent that stayed at the Ahwahnee and similar "Great Lodges," funds became available to build and maintain the National Parks for all to enjoy.

Although state-of-the-art technology was used to fireproof the Ahwahnee, it was camouflaged, like the cast concrete beams with molded wood grain stained to look like redwood. Rubber tile and glass were patterned in styles reminiscent of ancient Indian basketry, while giving clean lines meant to enhance and not detract from the impressive views.

Today, all visitors can relax and enjoy afternoon tea in the Great Lounge of the Ahwahnee. Although famed photographer Ansel Adams no longer entertains visitors with his other, lesser-known talent as a pianist, it is still a wonderful place to relax and absorb the beauty and elegance of Yosemite.

Adams is also attributed with helping to keep alive the lighthearted, elegant, musical Christmas extravaganza known as the Bracebridge Dinner held at the Ahwahnee on Christmas Eve, once he had graduated from being the court jester.

Begun in 1928, this reenactment of an 18th century English Feast has become a tradition that now spreads over five nights to accommodate the many guests celebrating what Andrea Fulton, the musical director, called, "... the Christmas that never was, but a Christmas that lives in everyone's heart."

11) Yosemite Falls V3

"This noble fall has far the richest, as well as the most powerful, voice of all the falls of the valley" said John Muir in The Yosemite in 1912.

John Muir was an explorer, an inventor, a scientist, a writer and a conservationist. Born in Scotland in 1838, his family moved to a Wisconsin farm in 1849. Muir did not complete his studies in botany, geology or literature at the University of Wisconsin, but eventually demonstrated far greater acuity in each of these subjects than many who had. Muir did well at whatever he laid his hands to, which kept him from his true pursuits until an industrial accident temporarily blinded him. In his memoirs he wrote, "I bade adieu to all my mechanical inventions, determined to devote the rest of my life to the study of the inventions of God."

In 1868, his travels led him to Yosemite. Yosemite Falls was considered by Muir to be one of Nature's "choicest treasures." Its variable voice is created by "comets" of water plummeting a sheer 1,430 feet on the upper fall, cascading merrily 675 feet on the middle fall, and finishing the show with an impressive mist-generating 320 feet on the final fall.

The total 2,425-foot drop is over 20 times the height of Niagara Falls, and has the distinction of being the fifth highest free-falling waterfall in the world.

Muir's cabin was located at the base of Yosemite Falls, and these falls piqued Muir's curiosity more than once. In one adventure, he climbed to the top of the falls, shimmied along the rushing water channel and peered down into the churning waters below. In another, he climbed a narrow shelf behind the torrent and caught glimpses of the moon through the thundering shower. Even in winter he was drawn to the falls to peer down into the "ice cone" which forms at its base and can reach over 300 feet in height. These activities were very dangerous and would not be recommended for anyone other than Muir!

Although Muir spent some time as a sheepherder, working at Hutching's sawmill, and managing a fruit farm while raising his family, his true life work was in understanding and protecting the flora, fauna and geology of American natural wonders all the way from Wisconsin, to Florida, to California and Alaska. The Sierra Club, founded in 1892, carries on Muir's proud tradition as documented at the LeConte Memorial Lodge.

12) Tunnel View W2

One of the signature views of Yosemite Valley, Tunnel View is situated at the end of Wawona Tunnel. At eight-tenths of a mile long, Wawona Tunnel is the longest in the Valley and cost over a million dollars to build in 1933. Early evening is a favorite time for people to gather here, whether professional photographer or first-time tourist. As the sun sets, the colors deepen and the magnificent scene is drenched in a golden-red alpenglow.

From this vantage point, it is easy to see why the resident Indians called Yosemite Valley "Ahwahnee" or "place of the gaping mouth." The "Gates of Yosemite," Cathedral Rocks on the right and El Capitan on the left, frame the wide gape of the deep valley with the magnificent profile of Half Dome and the shimmering flanks of Cloud's Rest at the far end of the valley.

Cloud's Rest is befittingly named. As the highest mountain visible at 9,926 feet, it appears to catch the clouds and hold them for a while, whether they are simple wisps on a sunny day, or massive and heavy with snow or rain. Imagine how Lord Bunnel of the Mariposa Battalion must have felt seeing the valley for the first time about 1,000 feet above this spot: "The grandeur of the scene was but softened by the haze that hung over the valley, light as gossamer, and by the clouds which partially dimmed the higher cliffs and mountains."

From Thomas Ayre's earliest sketches to Ansel Adam's photography, there has been a desire to capture the beauty of the valley so that it may be revisited anytime. Many of the early artists were also paid for their work in order to promote the valley and encourage more tourists to come. John Muir was just one of many reportedly drawn to the valley by the nationally distributed paintings.

Each artist developed a unique style to help set them apart from the others. The nostalgic appearance of Thomas Moran's paintings, while not precise in the finest details, captured the mood of a place so well that his paintings of Yellowstone and the Grand Canyon were the first by an American artist to be hung in the Capitol Building in Washington, D.C. Restoration of the Chris Jorgensen watercolors and oil paintings of California missions and Yosemite was begun 100 years after Norwegian-born Jorgensen first pitched his tent in Yosemite. These works and others by Hill, Keith, Bierstadt and Moran, to name a few, are featured at the Yosemite Museum in Yosemite Village.

The Ansel Adams studio in the village also continues to display historic as well as contemporary works of art. Although photography accurately captures the finest details of a setting, capturing its true essence on film is more sublime. Ansel Adams stated, "Sometimes I think I do get to places just when God's ready to have somebody click the shutter."

13) Chinquapin W5

As you travel the road from Yosemite to Wawona, notice the "old growth" forests of ponderosa, lodgepole, and fir, with some trees more than 40 inches in circumference and hundreds of years old. In the early 1920's, an inclined logging railway ran 3,500 feet straight down the west side of Henness Ridge. As cars loaded with the old growth lumber went down, unloaded cars were pulled up.

You may also see where a lightning strike in 1990 destroyed some of these old growth forests and caused more than 8,000 acres to burn in this region. In other areas of the park, the A-rock and Steamboat fires covered 18,100 and 5,280 acres respectively, including some loss of homes in Foresta. In the burned regions where trees have been destroyed, you can see the reclamation process taking place with grasses and shrubs encroaching upon the burned regions, and then smaller trees taking root.

The Indians controlled their environment by using proto-agricultural techniques such as pruning, selective harvesting, and burning. Fire was their most important tool for clearing brush, maintaining meadows, and reducing fuel accumulation that might otherwise sustain intense fires. Use of fire by American Indians diversified the habitat, and with an increased awareness and understanding of these ancient techniques, current land managers are successfully re-integrating fire into the ecosystem, through the use of prescribed burns.

Blood red bilberry grows in the cracks of boulders, and chinquapin, an evergreen shrub about 4 feet high, can be found on warm, open slopes between 3,000 and 8,000 feet. It is differentiated from the greenleaf manzanita which has shredded maroon bark, small apple-shaped berries, and leaves which are green on both sides. Chinquapin is related to the American chestnut, has a burr-like fruit, and leaves which are green on top and yellow underneath. The intersection with the road to Glacier Point at approximately 6,000 feet is named after this specialized plant.

Some of the animals which have adapted to the diversified forests between Yosemite Valley and Mariposa Grove include the pocket gopher, gopher snake, and mountain king snake, enemy of the rattlesnake, with distinguishing red, black and yellow stripes. Porcupines, which like the soft cambium inside lodgepole pines, are also found in this region. During autumn, acorns from the black oak provide another important food source for animals such as raccoons. Reminiscent of the real bandits, such as Black Bart who robbed stage coaches along this route in the early days, masked desperado raccoons are also known to go after your stuff, so keep your picnic areas and campsites clean!

14) Glacier Point & Half Dome G11

As you look at Half Dome and the gorgeous vista spread out 3,214 feet below the Jeffrey pines at Glacier Point, notice how wide, deep and flat-bottomed the valley is here. It is U-shaped compared to the narrow V-shape at the west end of the valley where the Merced River flows out. Notice also that the valleys from which the falls tumble are stranded high-up on Yosemite Valley's walls; and last but not least notice how the flanks of North Dome, Basket Dome and Cloud's Rest glisten in the sun.

Today this is appreciated as classic, glacial topography, carved by "rivers of ice," but when John Muir proposed his ideas, Josiah Whitney, California's state geologist, thought him a raving sheepherder. Whitney believed the valley was formed in a more cataclysmic manner, the popular belief at that time. Like the rocks themselves, some of the theories on the origin of Yosemite Valley have not stood the test of time and have simply eroded away, while others, even if not the complete story, have provided a bedrock upon which latter researchers could build.

Muir's insight provided this: "Nature chose for a tool, not the earthquake or lightning to rend and split asunder, not stormy torrent or eroding rain, but the tender snow-flowers noiselessly falling through unnumbered centuries."

It takes about 100 feet of snow to create enough weight to cause the outward ice flow at the bottom of the glacier. Imagine the immensity of the ice, over 5,500 feet, it took to fill and carve these valleys. At least three periods of glaciation have been identified in Yosemite Valley, beginning with the Pre-Tahoe about two to three million years ago and peaking about 15,000 to 20,000 years ago during the Tioga Glaciation.

Two rivers of ice converged at this point and moved imperceptibly westward, bulldozing sediments beneath its snout and carrying train-loads of boulders on its crevassed back. The uneven pressure, and freezing and thawing of ice in cracks and joints in the rocks along the margins of the ice, quarried more rocks with which to scour and polish the valley and left behind the classic steep walls of the U-shaped valley.

When the climate warmed and the glacier melted, the streams stranded high on the valley walls now leapt freely, as unencumbered, magnificent waterfalls, into a pristine lake which had formed behind a dam-like glacial moraine of rock and dirt left behind by the receding glacier. Eventually, the sediments from the streams and rivers filled in the lake, creating the fertile, flat meadows on the valley floor and the streams started to erode back into the valley walls forming side canyons and adding musical cascades to the waterfalls.

15) Wawona W10

Wawona rolls off the tongue like the idyllic rolling forested hills and meadows, which it names. Woh-woh'-nah is an Indian imitation of an owl's hooting sound and means "big tree." The Indians believed an owl to be the guardian spirit and deity of the big trees, the sequoias, and Wawona is known to be one of the wintering areas for the great grey owl.

The grand, balconied hotel in this country-like setting was called the "Big Tree Station," until its name was officially changed to the Wawona Hotel in 1882. In the 1850's, the station began when Galen Clark homesteaded 160 acres at a former Indian encampment almost exactly halfway between the Mariposa Grove and Yosemite Valley. The station was sold to the Yankee Washburn brothers in 1874, who built the covered bridge reminiscent of their home in Vermont over the south fork of the Merced. The Washburn brothers completed the stage coach road from Wawona to Yosemite Valley and began building the lodging facilities shortly thereafter.

As tourism grew in the valley, Wawona also bloomed with tourist attractions. The hotel complex grew and included dancing, tennis, swimming, golf, photography studios, and soda fountains in addition to other amenities. In 1932, the National Park Service took over the oldest resort complex in California and Wawona was declared a National Historic Landmark in 1987. Victorian-style lodging is still offered today and meals are served in the Wawona Hotel dining room, decorated with the photography of Carleton Watkins.

The Pioneer History Museum was created at Wawona utilizing local highlights, such as the covered bridge, and historic buildings from other areas of the park, like the "Old Village," to preserve the culture of bygone eras. Rangers in costume, stagecoach rides, a jail, working blacksmith, wagons, antique farm machinery and mining equipment from the Benettville Silver Mine add to the ambiance.

Birds and animals also enjoy this pastoral setting and you may be fortunate enough to spot an endangered Willow Flycatcher, or hear the splendid glissade of the red-winged blackbird as you stroll on the Wawona Meadow trail. Peaking in June are flowering redbud, Sierra onion, lupine, and Mariposa Lily, so named because its purple-tinged, white-winged petals resemble the wings of a butterfly, which, in Spanish, is "mariposa". Along the river, you may spot an American dipper, bopping in and out of the cool water, or even walking upstream, under water, clinging to the rocks while in search of food.

Along the Chilnualna Fall Trail, which offers the panoramic scenery of the Merced's south fork, the Wawona Dome, and cascading falls, you may see dark-eyed juncos, chipping sparrows or lodgepole chipmunks competing for incense cedar seeds. In shady moist areas, Sierra shooting star can be found. Mountain Misery, the plant with oozing black, sticky gum, was used by the Indians as a salve for "skin eruption" diseases such as acne, chicken pox, and measles.

16) Mariposa Grove S1

Born of fire, the Giant Sequoias sprout from seeds smaller than a sesame seed. Bristlecone pines in California's White Mountains may be older, and the Coastal Redwoods may be taller, but no other living plant has the combined height and breadth of the Giant Sequoias. Mariposa Grove has the famous Grizzly Giant, one of the two largest sequoias in Yosemite, with a volume of almost 1,000 cubic meters and a weight that has been estimated at about 2 million pounds. The most common age reported for the Grizzly is 2,700 years old, but more recent scientific estimates have placed the age closer to 1,700 years old. Its grizzled appearance comes not so much from its age as from lightening strikes and the loss of bark at its base. If you look closely, you may spot a mule deer buck that has made his home in the wood caves formed at base of the Grizzly Giant.

When you look at the Clothespin Tree and fire scars on some of the other trees in the grove, it is hard to imagine these trees actually needing fire to survive, but it is a complex system that has evolved over centuries. Squirrel-like chickarees nest in the green branches of the sequoias, eat the flower buds, forget where some of the cones are buried, and thereby inadvertently plant a tree.

Fire enriches the soil and clears the underbrush so the seedlings can grow freely. The fire also chars the bark and opens crevasses in the massive sequoias for new wildlife to shelter and begin the cycle.

The trees have evolved a fibrous outer bark, up to two inches thick, which efficiently shields them from most fires. In addition, the trees can heal lesser wounds by re-growing outer bark over them. Even when the damage is significant and it seems the tree should die, the extensive root system can pull in nutrients to keep it going, provided the soil is loose and untrampled above them. This explains why the large areas around the base of the trees are fenced off.

In the Mariposa Grove, there are over 500 mature sequoias, making it one of the largest reserves from among the 75 groves in the Sierra. Fortunately, Galen Clark recognized the uniqueness and value of these trees he first saw in 1857, and together with Milton Mann, worked to preserve them. Through a collective effort, the Yosemite Grant was enacted and signed into law by Abraham Lincoln in 1864, setting a positive, lasting precedent for the formation of parks to preserve natural wonders. From 1866 to 1880, Galen Clark was the first Guardian of the Grant, but today every visitor can be a custodian, preserving Yosemite National Park for future generations.

17) Tuolumne Grove O1

This grove of Giant Sequoias, also known as Sierra Redwoods, may have been the one mentioned in the memoirs of the Walker Party, the first Euro-Americans to have entered this region. The Walker Party was a group of about 50 trappers who split off from Captain Bonneville in the Rockies in 1833 and almost starved to death in the snows of the Sierras on their journey to the West Coast.

The Giant Sequoias only grow in isolated groups at high snowy elevations between 5,000 and 8,000 feet. The elevation for this grove, which is about 1/10th of a mile down the old Oak Flat Road, is 5,730 feet. There are approximately 25 trees in this tract, including the remnants of a Tunnel Tree which was cut in 1878.

In the 1930's, the Rockefeller Foundation and the federal government bought large tracts of land which were added to Yosemite Park and included part of the Tuolumne Grove to help preserve the sugar pines as well as the sequoias.

The large cones, up to 2 feet long, found in Tuolumne Grove are sometimes thought to belong to the sequoia, but in fact belong to the sugar pines. Sugar pines have ridged, red-brown or gray bark and needles in sets of five.

Incense cedars are sometimes confused with the sequoias, that is, until the sequoias become old enough and large enough to set themselves apart. Infant sequoias do not resemble their parents as they are triangular in shape with drooping, bluish, evergreen branches from ground to tip. When the tree is 10 to 30 years old, it begins to develop a pole-like bare trunk and roots that grow out laterally. Then, the branches stop drooping, thicken up, and form elbows as the foliage becomes a darker green. By the time a sequoia is a couple of thousand years old, its bark is a deep, reddish-brown, covering trunks 20 feet or more in diameter and branches which are as big as small trees.

The oldest trees are not necessarily the largest and vice versa, making the age difficult to estimate from size alone, although that is still the easiest and most often used method to approximate the age. Two of the oldest known trees, the Cleveland and Washington, in the Giant Forest at Sequoia National Park have been estimated to be 3,000 to 4,000 years old.

No one can say it any better than Muir: "We all travel the milky way together, trees and men ... I beheld the countless hosts of the forests, hushed and tranquil, towering above one another on the slopes of the hills like a devout audience. The setting sun filled them with amber light, and seemed to say, My peace I give unto you."

18) Olmsted Point & Tenaya Lake T24

From Olmsted Point you can peer up Tenaya Canyon to see Tenaya Lake, or down it and see the granite flanks of Cloud's Rest and Half Dome, which were sculpted by the Tenaya Glacier. According to John McPhee, author of the award-winning Basin and Range, geologists say "granodiorite when they are in church and granite the rest of the week!"

Granites are light colored, grayish-pink rocks. Granodiorite has more dark colored, "mafic" crystals and is higher in iron or magnesium, than granite. Quartz diorite's dark color comes from an even greater number of mafic crystals. Individual rocks of the granite family can be anywhere in between granite and quartz diorite, and geologists have carefully named and categorized each brother, sister and cousin.

They are all plutonic rocks, named after Pluto, the Roman god of the underworld, because the molten lava from which they formed never made it to the surface of the earth. When one piece of the earth's crust was pushed under another, it melted and the molten lava ballooned up toward the surface, but was trapped and cooled in place. Large crystals in the rocks means the lava cooled slowly. Sometimes the light colored crystals are extremely large, a few inches long.

The collection of 80-200 million year old plutons throughout the Sierra Nevada created a "batholith" (from the Greek words bathos, meaning deep and lithos, meaning rock). So how did these granites, which formed hidden beneath a thick layer of 500 million year old rocks, become exposed to scouring by glaciers? As one plate of the earth's crust pushed under another, the rocks were lifted up. What goes up must come down, and the overlying rocks were simply eroded away.

Of course, so much change does not come without stress, and 15-25 million years ago a fault formed along the eastern edge of the Sierra Nevada which allowed the whole Sierra block of rocks to tilt toward the Pacific Ocean, accelerating erosion. Glaciers took advantage of preexisting stream valleys and weak spots in the rocks to erode and form the broad valleys apparent today.

Sometimes the boulders at the bottom of the glacier gouged the underlying rock forming "glacial striations," and sometimes they were left behind as "glacial erratics." In other places, finer sediments at the base of the glaciers smoothed the granite escarpments, creating the "glacial polish" that brilliantly reflects the sun. Excellent examples of this are seen on the escarpments of Cloud's Rest and near Tenaya Lake, which the Indians called Py-wi-ack for "lake of the shining rocks."

At 8,149 feet, the Tenaya branch of Tuolumne Glacier excavated the mile long and ½ mile wide lake basin, making Tenaya Lake one of the largest and highest lakes in the park.

Top - Tenaya Lake Reflections
Bottom - Olmsted Point View

19) Tuolumne Meadows T29

One of the largest subalpine meadows in the Sierra Nevada is Tuolumne Meadows. Here the Dana and Lyell Forks of the Tuolumne River, sometimes milky with glacial flour, fine grained sediments from upstream glaciers, combine before flowing down to Hetch Hetchy Valley. Lembert Dome, named for a sheepherder and homesteader who lived here in the 1880's, can be seen across the meadow, its glacial polished and plucked roche moutonnee profile silhouetted against the darker red metamorphosed volcanic rocks of Mount Dana and Mount Gibbs.

Several trails allow one to enjoy the geologic features and natural beauty of this area, including the Soda Springs Trail. Along the way are spectacular views of the river, meadows, and mountains, including Unicorn Peak. Imagine this horn of rock sticking forlornly above a sea of ice and resisting glacial erosion. The Soda Springs Trail takes you on an easy stroll through meadows with marmots, lilies, and robins; past the naturally carbonated springs with their rich red mud; to a pioneer cabin and to the Parsons Memorial Lodge built in 1914.

One of the people who had the vision to preserve and protect Yosemite's beautiful meadows was Theodore "Teddy" Roosevelt. Teddy came to know and love the Yosemite Valley with the help of good friends like John Muir. As United States President from 1901-1909, Teddy Roosevelt unified the Yosemite Valley and Mariposa Grove, integrating both into the greater Yosemite National Park. He also increased the number of national parks from five to ten and increased the area of the forest reserves by over 400%, to an area approximately the size of all the Atlantic states from Maine to Virginia and larger than the area of France, Belgium, and the Netherlands combined.

Thirty years later, his cousin, Franklin Delano Roosevelt, took action to both protect the lands and environment, and to try and bring hope back to a troubled nation with thousands of unemployed men. Within 37 days of his inauguration, the first of over 600,000 men were employed in "Roosevelt's Tree Army," the Civilian Conservation Corps. The roads and stone bridges built by the Army Corps of Engineers in the early 1900's, in accordance with Major H.C. Benson's plan, were now complimented by new structures built by the CCC, such as the Half Dome Cable system and the Badger Pass Ski complex. They created a lasting legacy in sweat and stone as the nation tried to recover from the most severe economic depression it had known.

The National Civilian Conservation Corps lacked funding to continue its existence and its work during World War II, but today there is still a CCC taking care of Yosemite. The California Conservation Corps carries out trail building and maintenance chores that preserve, protect, and enhance Yosemite National Park.

Top - Tuolumne Meadows
Bottom - Soda Springs Area

20) Tioga Pass & Lakes T39

At 9,941 feet, Tioga Pass is the highest automobile pass in California. The road was originally built to service the Benettville Silver Mine. Unfortunately, the Sheepherder Lode, the rich silver vein they were mining for, was never found. Today, however, the road leads many tourists to find treasures of a different kind, such as the beautiful sparkling lakes and the wildlife that abounds around them.

From Mono Lake, a remnant of the inland sea which captured the runoff of the ancient glaciers, to Tioga, Ellery, Tenaya, Siesta, and countless other tarn and kettle lakes between, the blue sparkling waters ripple with mountain breezes and wash away one's cares.

John Muir counted "... a grand total of 111 lakes whose waters come to sing at Yosemite. So glorious is the background of the great valley, so harmonious its relations to its wide-spreading fountains."

Tarn lakes form in the rock bowls called cirques carved at the head of a glacier. Kettle lakes form where large chunks of ice cleaved off the ice flow and then melted, leaving large holes in the glacial sediment which fill with water. The several small lakes near the Tioga Pass entrance are good examples of kettle lakes.

When the glacial lakes are strung in a line down a glaciated valley, they are also known as Pater Noster lakes for their resemblance to the beads of a rosary. Glacial moraines often act as dams, trapping a lake behind them, such as shown by Siesta Lake. As the lake fills with sediment, flat-bottomed valleys are formed, sometimes leaving a small lake, like Mirror Lake in Yosemite Valley, as a reminder of its grand glacial predecessor.

Abundant wildlife thrives around and within the lakes. The brine shrimp and alkali flies of salty Mono Lake attract large numbers of migratory birds and year-round waterfowl which perch upon the tufa towers. The tufa towers formed when calcium deposits from underwater springs were exposed as the salty inland lake, a sister to the Great Salt Lake of Utah, evaporated. Its high salt content is the result of no outlet so all the minerals which flow into it become highly concentrated and saturate the water.

The fresh waters of the upland glacial lakes attract birds, mammals, and man. The lakes, once cloudy with glacial flour, now are frequently crystal clear, showing the multihued stones on the lake bottoms and mirroring the landscape.

From May to September almost no rain falls in the high country, except for an occasional thunder-storm, so man and animals are dependent upon the water in the lakes, rivers and streams which comes from the winter snow melt. Early morning and evening are good times for photography because the low angle of the sun increases the reflections and wildlife often come to drink.

According to Muir, "And after ten years of wandering and wondering in the heart of it, rejoicing in its glorious floods of light, the white beams of the morning streaming through the passes, the noonday radiance on the crystal rocks, the flush of the alpenglow and the irised spray of countless waterfalls, it seems above all others the Range of Light."

May you take with you memories of Yosemite's beauty, the cascading falls, magnificent meadows, rippling rivers and lakes, dancing blooms, verdant wildlife and proud promontories and may they last a lifetime and be shared with generations to come.

Top - Lake Reflections near Tioga Entrance
Bottom - Mono Lake with Tufa Towers

21) Mirror Lake
V26

**22) Hetch Hetchy
Reservoir
H4**

23) San Francisco

Welcome to beautiful San Francisco, Fisherman's Wharf, and the San Francisco Maritime National Historical Park! The San Francisco Bay is the largest inlet on the California coast, covering an expanse 60 miles long and 12 miles wide. Actually an estuary containing a mix of fresh and salt water, the San Francisco Bay is fed by 16 rivers that flow through it and out into the Pacific Ocean. The composition of the bay is what causes the famed San Francisco fog. When a northwesterly wind blows in from the coast, it stirs up the California current. This current mixes with the warm air on the surface and forms the fog. Home to several microclimates, the 49 square miles of San Francisco are largely unpredictable, and it is not uncommon to experience a change in temperature from one street to the next. Mark Twain is said to have observed, "The coldest winter I ever spent was a summer in San Francisco."

The most visible landmark in this area is the Golden Gate Bridge, which traverses the two miles between the bay's coasts and connects the Marin headlands to San Francisco. Construction was completed in 1937 and, at that time, it was the longest suspension bridge in the world. Its twin suspension towers each measure 746 feet and were the highest of any structure west of New York City. Despite the competition from the larger and more trafficked Bay Bridge, which connects San Francisco and Oakland, Golden Gate Bridge remains the icon of the San Francisco Bay.

During the gold rush of the mid-1800's, San Francisco was home to people from all four corners of the earth hoping to strike it rich. It was this diverse population that has given this area its unique and colorful flavor. Rich with history, culture and excitement, San Francisco is legendary, and definitely a one-of-a-kind experience.

24) San Francisco Wharf & Maritime Park

At the west end of Fisherman's Wharf is the unique San Francisco Maritime National Historical Park where you can explore America's only floating National Park by climbing aboard historic vessels at the Hyde Street Pier, gaze at the bay from the control deck atop the boat-shaped Maritime Museum, or even take a break from the bay front breezes and step back in time among the exhibits at the Visitor Center. The Argonaut Hotel just to the west of the Cannery shares the old Cannery warehouse with the Maritime Park Visitor Center. The national historic register building belongs to the National Park Service, and was developed under an historic leasing program.

At the Visitor Center you can see the light from the Farallon Lighthouse on display. The Farallon Lighthouse was built in 1855, and its 280,000 candlepower light illuminated the coast during the busy time following the gold rush, when clipper ships and other sea-faring vessels were sailing into San Francisco Bay in large numbers. Eight thick prisms refracted the light as far as 26 miles across the dangerous waters of the Bay.

Not all ships were fortunate enough to see the light, however, as shown by the shipwreck also on display at the visitor center.

Before you leave the Visitor Center, check out the models of the ships anchored at Hyde Street Pier, as well as their commemorative national historic "landmark" plaques. Hyde Street Pier has one of the world's largest collections of historic ships, and many of the ships docked here played a role in San Francisco history, including the 1886 square-rigged sailing ship Balclutha, the 1890 ferryboat Eureka and the 1891 Alma Scow Schooner. The park also boasts a collection of more than 100 traditional and significant small craft, from shrimp junks to sloop yachts.

As you stroll along the pier, take your time and enjoy this testament to the American maritime tradition. Listen to the rigging of each ship as it gently sways on the water. Take a boat building class, learn to sing a sea chantey or watch school children learn to tie ship-worthy knots. This interactive collection brings you into a bygone age, and lets you discover the art of boatbuilding and the history of the sailors who lived and worked aboard these magnificent vessels.

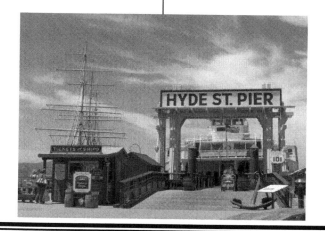

Waypoint Tours®

Plan, Enhance & Cherish
Your Travel Adventures!

This Waypoint Tour® is your
personal tour guide unlocking the
fascinating highlights, history,
geology & nature of
Yosemite National Park.

Waypoint Tours® are entertaining,
educational, self-guided tours to help
plan your travel adventures,
enhance your travel experience &
cherish your travel memories.

Travel Destinations include:
Bryce Canyon UT
Grand Canyon South Rim AZ
Grand Teton WY
Mount McKinley Denali AK
North Rim Grand Canyon AZ
Rocky Mountains CO
San Antonio TX
San Diego CA
San Francisco CA
San Francisco Wharf & Maritime Park
Sedona AZ
Washington DC
Yellowstone WY
Yosemite CA
Zion UT

Tour Guide Books Plus DVD & MP3s
Tour Road Guides Plus Audio CDs
Tour Guide Books
DVD & CD Complete Tour Packages
DVD Tour Guides
DVD Tour Postcards

These Tour Solutions Plus More at
www.waypointtours.com
tours@waypointtours.com

Highlights, History, Geology,
Nature & More!

Credits

Book by Waypoint Tours
Editing by Waypoint Tours
Photography by Waypoint Tours
Original Tour by Laurie Ann
Maps & Photo on page 32 by the
National Park Service

Special thanks to the
Yosemite Association & the
Yosemite National Park Service.

Support Yosemite National Park
with a membership to:

Yosemite Association
P.O. Box 230
El Portal, California 95318
(209) 379-2646
yosemite.org

Yosemite National Park Service
P.O. Box 577
Yosemite, CA 95389
(209) 372-0200
www.nps.gov/yose

Leave No Trace

Optional Audio CD Contents

Audio CD Driving Tour (75 min)

Optional DVD-ROM Contents

DVD Narrated Tour (45 min)
MP3 Audio Tour (75 min)
PC Multimedia Screensaver
Digital Photo Gallery

Breathtaking Photography,
Professional Narration &
Beautiful Orchestration

DVD Plays Worldwide in
All Regions
Mastered in HDV in English
* Denotes Waypoints on DVD
PC Multimedia Screensaver &
Digital Photo Gallery Each Contain
100+ High-Resolution Photos

Professional Voicing by
Janet Ault & Mark Andrews
Recording by Audiomakers, Inc.
For private non-commercial use only
Detailed info & credits on
DVD-ROM

Optional CD & DVD-ROM Info

Track #) Title

1) Yosemite*
2) Bridalveil Fall* W1
3) El Capitan &
   Bridalveil View* V14
4) Sentinel Rock &
   Four-Mile Trail V18
5) Sentinel Bridge &
   Cooks Meadow*
6) Curry Village V22
7) Happy Isles & Waterfalls V24
8) Stoneman Meadow &
   Royal Arches* V23
9) Yosemite Village V1
10) Ahwahnee Lodge*
11) Yosemite Falls* V3
12) Tunnel View W2
13) Chinquapin W5
14) Glacier Point & Half Dome* G11
15) Wawona W10
16) Mariposa Grove* S1
17) Tuolumne Grove O1
18) Olmsted Point &
    Tenaya Lake* T24
19) Tuolumne Meadows* T29
20) Tioga Pass & Lakes* T39

W1, W14, etc. Correspond to
Park Roadside Markers

Notes

51792436R00039

Made in the USA
San Bernardino, CA
01 August 2017